Chickens

Judy Wearing

![W] **WEIGL PUBLISHERS INC.**
"Creating Inspired Learning"
www.weigl.com

Published by Weigl Publishers Inc.
350 5th Avenue, 59th Floor
New York, NY 10118
Website: www.weigl.com

Library of Congress Cataloging-in-Publication Data

Wearing, Judy.
 Chickens / Judy Wearing.
    p. cm. -- (Watch them grow)
 Includes bibliographical references and index.
 ISBN 978-1-60596-913-8 (hard cover : alk. paper) -- ISBN 978-1-60596-914-5 (soft cover : alk. paper) --
 ISBN 978-1-60596-915-2 (e-book)
 1. Chicks--Juvenile literature. 2. Chickens--Development--Juvenile literature. 3. Eggs--Juvenile literature. I. Title.
 SF498.4.W43 2011
 636.5'07--dc22

                              2009050943

Printed in the United States of America in North Mankato, Minnesota
1 2 3 4 5 6 7 8 9 0 14 13 12 11 10

042010
WEP264000

Editor: Heather C. Hudak
Design: Terry Paulhus

All of the Internet URLs given in the book were valid at the time of publication. However, due to the dynamic nature of the Internet, some addresses may have changed, or sites may have ceased to exist since publication. While the author and publisher regret any inconvenience this may cause readers, no responsibility for any such changes can be accepted by either the author or the publisher.

Every reasonable effort has been made to trace ownership and to obtain permission to reprint copyright material. The publishers would be pleased to have any errors or omissions brought to their attention so that they may be corrected in subsequent printings.

Weigl acknowledges Getty Images as its primary image supplier for this title.

CONTENTS

4   What is a Chicken?

7   Exciting Eggs

8   Keeping Warm

10 Breaking Free

13 Balls of Fluff

14 Growing Up

16 Hens and Roosters

19 Scratch and Peck

20 Backyards and Barns

22 Decorate an Egg

23 Find Out More

24 Glossary/Index

What is a Chicken?

Have you ever seen a bird with a **crest** on its head and skin flaps under its beak? This may have been a chicken. There are more than 170 kinds of chickens. Chickens have two legs, two wings, and a beak. They can be black, white, brown, or a mix of colors. Female chickens are called hens. Male chickens are called roosters.

Like all animals, chickens have a life cycle. They hatch, grow, and lay eggs.

Chickens are thought to be the closest living relatives to *Tyrannosaurus rex*.

Exciting Eggs

Did you know that more than 80 billion eggs are laid in the United States each year? A hen can lay as many as 300 eggs a year. Eggs only hatch into chicks if the hen mates with a rooster.

In nature, hens only lay eggs until fall. This is when days get shorter and colder. On farms, hens lay eggs year round. Farmers use lights to make the days seem longer.

Farmers shine a light on eggs to see if there is a chick inside. A dark lump will show through the shell if there is a chick inside.

Keeping Warm

Why do hens sit on their eggs? Hens sit on their eggs to keep them warm. This helps the chick inside grow. The hen uses her beak to turn the eggs often. This keeps the chicks from sticking to one side of the shell.

Inside the egg, the growing chick feeds on the **yolk**. Its heart starts beating on its first day in the egg. The egg white acts as a pillow for the chick. The hard shell keeps the chick safe.

The shell has 17,000 tiny holes. The holes let air and water pass through the egg.

Breaking Free

Did you know that chicks make peeping sounds when they are ready to leave the egg? Chicks are ready to hatch about 21 days after the egg is laid. They tap their beak against the shell and poke a hole. Then, chicks tap around the shell to break it into two parts. It can take a chick as long as 24 hours to hatch out of its egg.

Chicks are wet when they hatch. Their **down** dries quickly. Chicks stay under their mother for a day or two after they hatch. This keeps them safe and warm.

Balls of Fluff

Have you ever seen a baby bird that looks like a fluffy yellow ball? Chicks have soft, yellow feathers to keep them warm. They have small wings and a small beak.

A group of chicks is called a peep. They make a peep noise so their mother can find them. In nature, chicks stay with their mother for about six weeks.

Chicks do not need to eat or drink for three days after they hatch. They feed off yolk that is in their stomach.

Growing Up

When do chicks become chickens? Chicks begin to look more like chickens at three to six months. They lose their fluffy down and grow adult feathers. At about five months, female chickens can begin to lay eggs. They can lay one egg per day.

Chickens are full-grown at 32 weeks of age. Adult chickens weigh between 1.25 and 12 pounds (0.6 and 5.4 kilograms).

According to the *Guinness World Book of Records*, the oldest chicken lived to be 16 years of age.

Hens and Roosters

Do you have a comb for your hair? Chickens also have a comb. It is a tuft of skin that sticks up from the top of their head. Combs come in many shapes and sizes. The combs of most chickens are red.

The flap of skin under a chicken's chin is called a **wattle**. Roosters have a bigger comb and wattle than hens. Roosters also have long tail feathers.

Scratch and Peck

How would you chew your food without any teeth? Chickens do not have teeth. Instead, they have a small **sac** of stones inside their throat. The stones help the chicken grind its food into tiny pieces.

Grains, insects, worms, and vegetables are some of the foods chickens eat. They scratch the ground with their feet to find their food. Then, they peck at it with their beak.

Many chickens have yellow legs. Their legs will be more yellow if they eat foods that are yellow.

Backyards and Barns

Do you have a pet dog or cat? Some people keep chickens as pets. In fact, chickens were some of the world's first tamed animals. Today, most chickens in North America live on farms.

People in China began keeping chickens about 8,000 years ago.

Decorate an Egg

Supplies

hard-boiled eggs

white glue

basket

rice, grains, spices

popcorn

egg carton

newspaper

1. Lay a sheet of newspaper on a work table. Hold an egg in one hand with the top showing.

2. Rub a thin layer of glue on the top of the egg.

3. Gently put spices, grains, or rice onto the glue. Try making shapes, such as stars or stripes.

4. Put the egg into the egg carton to dry for one hour.

5. Hold the egg by the top part that has been decorated. Repeat steps 2 to 4.

6. Decorate many eggs, and arrange them in a basket.

Find Out More

To learn more about chickens, visit these websites.

Life Cycle of a Chicken
www.vtaide.com/png/chicken.htm

All About Chickens
www.enchantedlearning.
com/subjects/birds/info/
chicken.shtml

**All About Chickens for Kids
and Teachers**
www.kiddyhouse.com/
Farm/Chicken

Kids' Farm
http://nationalzoo.si.edu/
Animals/KidsFarm/InTheBarn/
Chickens/default.cfm

Glossary

crest: a tuft of fur, skin, or feathers on the top of the head

down: soft feather tufts that cover the bodies of birds

sac: a baglike part of the body

wattle: the flap of skin under a chicken's chin

yolk: the yellow part of an egg that feeds the chick inside

Index

beak 4, 8, 10, 13, 19

chick 7, 8, 10, 13, 14

egg 4, 7, 8, 10, 14, 22

feathers 13, 14, 16
food 19

grow 4, 8, 14

hatch 4, 7, 10, 13
hen 4, 7, 8, 14, 16

rooster 4, 7, 16